Charming Unicorn

Shy Unicorn

UNICORNS

Lovely Unicorn

Sparkly Unicorn

UNICORNS

Rainbow Unicorn

Shiny
Unicorn

UNICORNS

Cute Unicorn

Sweet Unicorn

Funny
Unicorn

Amazing Unicorn

Pretty Unicorn

Flying Unicorn

Speedy Unicorn

Cool Unicorn

Beautiful
Unicorn

Hungry Unicorn

UNICORNS

Aurora Mermaid

Syrena Mermaid

MERMAIDS

Isla
Mermaid

Cora Mermaid

Nami Mermaid

MERMAIDS

Oceana Mermaid

Nerida Mermaid

MERMAIDS

Serena Mermaid

Ondine
Mermaid

MERMAIDS

Marina Mermaid

MERMAIDS

Finley Mermaid

Lily
Mermaid

MERMAIDS

Anemone Mermaid

Alana
Mermaid